LIKE A
Rolling Stone

LIKE A
Rolling Stone

The mad misadventures of two
English lads crossing America as
the Rolling Stones

Mark Howell

**The New
Atlantian Library**

THE NEW ATLANTIAN LIBRARY
is an imprint of
ABSOLUTELY AMAZING eBOOKS

Published by Whiz Bang LLC, 926 Truman Avenue, Key West, Florida 33040, USA.

Like a Rolling Stone copyright © 2014, 2015 by Mark Howell. Electronic compilation/ paperback edition copyright © 2015 by Whiz Bang LLC. A first iteration of this story appeared in serial form in *Konk Life*. Cover design: Judy Bullard. *Like a Rolling Stone* was previously published under the title of *The Naked Girl in the Treehouse*

All rights reserved. No part of this book may be reproduced, scanned, or transmitted in any form or by any means, electronic or mechanical, including photocopying, recording, or any information storage and retrieval system, without permission in writing from the publisher. Please do not participate in or encourage piracy of copyrighted materials in violation of the author's rights. Purchase only authorized ebook editions.

This is a work of fiction. Names, characters, places, and incidents either are the product of the author's imagination or are used fictitiously, and any resemblance to actual persons, living or dead, businesses, companies, events, or locales is entirely coincidental. While the author has made every effort to provide accurate information at the time of publication, neither the publisher nor the author assumes any responsibility for errors, or for changes that occur after publication. Further, the publisher does not have any control over and does not assume any responsibility for author or third-party websites or their contents. How the ebook displays on a given reader is beyond the publisher's control.

For information contact:
Publisher@AbsolutelyAmazingEbooks.com

ISBN-13: 978-0692576205 (New Atlantian Library, The)
ISBN-10: 0692576207

Dedicated to Jan, Rafael, Peter, Melissa, Jerry, Chase, Preston, Amanda, Amelia, Alec, Geoff, Naomi, Rhiannon, Logan, Gwendy, Steven, Bubba, Kiera-Bella, Sixto, Mike and Carrie, David Crigman and Shirrel Rhoades.

LIKE A
Rolling Stone

Chapter One

"All is true," I said, in fact the very first words I said to him, even as we launched ourselves into the biggest lie of our lives, which was actually the very best thing we could have done.

"I just can't believe it, in just a few days we'll be in America," he said, then added, "Hi, I'm David Carpenter."

"Hi," I said. "I'm Thom One." We shook hands and so it all began in the month of April 1964.

As cabin mates assigned to the bowels of the ship, we were two strangers connecting for the first time here in our windowless accommodation aboard the SS United States as this great transatlantic liner, launched a mere 12 years before, headed out from Southampton via the English Channel and the Strait of Dover and thence across the Atlantic at record speed on its way to New York City in the United States.

"All is True" was actually the title that Shakespeare gave his play about Henry the Eighth, although it might in fact have been written by someone called Kyd, so you see, David and I may well have been beset by matters of the truth right from the outset as we set out on our way to discover that a person's life can be just an act, after all.

It was on that inaugural night in our cramped and stuffy quarters, well below the waterline, even as the huge swells of wave upon wave throughout the Bay of Biscay suspended our supine spines above the neighboring bunks only to plunge us deeply back into our mattresses, that David and I came up with our first and only true difference of opinion.

We revealed a lot to each other that first night.

I was from Cheltenham, a small spa town in the west of England, and David was from Birmingham, an industrious city in the Midlands, but we were far too curious of each other at this point for any of that to make any difference. He had no brothers or sisters and seemed happy to be to be a loner. I had a twin brother and in spite of my last name of One I was forever seeking a number two.

We were both 18 and unavoidably headed to college at the end of the year, the reason our parents had packed us off to the New World so we wouldn't waste our days idling them away at home.

The fact was that we were both already in love with America. David was off to law school in the autumn and wanted a big adventure before that happened. I was supposed to be going to Cambridge on a scholarship but I didn't really want to because I had a girlfriend in my hometown and anyway I'd already fallen in love with Jack Kerouac. Somehow amidst all of that, I really wanted to enter the church.

"What's your girlfriend's name?" asked David.

"Mary," I said. "She's the vicar's daughter."

"That's a very religious name," he said.

"So is David Carpenter, if you think about it," I said.

From the way he then went on about all the girls he knew in Birmingham, including two called Mary, I took it he was not a virgin.

I couldn't say the same about myself but I did tell him that Mary's favorite record was Connie Francis singing "I Worry and Wonder." He seemed not impressed, so I told him, "Hey, there's Freud and Jung right there."

"I don't get it," he said.

But the difference of opinion was this:

Like a Rolling Stone

    David thought the Rolling Stones were, as he put it, cool, although they hadn't even hit the U.S. yet while I considered the Beatles, who were already a huge hit in America, to be, in a word groovy, a word I'd continue to use for much of the rest of my life.

Chapter 2

The next morning, April 1, the one thing on each of our minds it turned out was no fool but the fact that the dead body of the president of the United States, John Fitzgerald Kennedy, lay still fresh in his grave.

So we decided to rush directly upstairs to meet some American passengers sure to be aboard.

Breakfast was served to the mass of passengers in the vast main dining hall — first-class not allowed— and that was where we immediately laid our eyes on (all is true!) twenty or more female students who, within seconds, informed us they were from Lake Erie College in Painesville, Ohio and headed back to school from their winter trip to London.

The fascination went both ways. David and I gaped at them. "Is this a bevy?" he murmured to me as they beckoned us to sit down at one of their tables.

David and I wore identical gray wool sweaters and corduroy pants. The girls were dressed in a blaze of colored shirts and denim blue jeans.

Collectively they called us Brits and we called them Yanks, but by the end of that first breakfast we had discovered that to, a person, they agreed with us that the Sixties, despite a rocky start in Dallas, were going to be *so good!* By the end of the meal David and I had each selected which of the Painesville girls would be our particular friend during the remainder of the voyage and maybe even beyond it.

The truth was that the entire trip would pass in a blur, in the blink of an eye. And yet, how can one forget? Two of the first-class voyagers aboard this already fabled vessel were the equally fabled Duke and Duchess of Windsor, whom we and a couple of the girls would actually glimpse during one of our forays into the first-class lounge.

More importantly, aboard with us among the passenger class were two young guys just graduated from Cambridge who sang and played guitar and were headed for Las Vegas to join the Jackie Mason show as backup entertainers. These were the fellows who'd go on to become lifetime entertainers, Hendra as editor of the National Lampoon plus that famously hilarious turn as the band's agent in the movie "Spinal Tap" among other achievements; and Nick Ullett who also became a transatlantic musician and actor. Hendra was the weird one, able to sleep while lying on the floor with his eyes half open so he could grab the ankles of passing kids and startle them half to death.

It was Ullett and Hendra who got us all singing on the deck of the ship. Ullett was terrific on the guitar, much appreciated by David, who'd brought his own guitar with him to America, while Hendra knew the words to all the Beatles' songs, which was deeply appreciated by me.

Looking back, of course, we came to realize that it was this pair, more even than the girls from Painesville, who truly inspired us to do what we did on our trip across America, leading a number of today's American mothers and housewives to still believe they were once serenaded by two of the Rolling Stones.

But that all was yet to come (God bless our immortal souls for simply giving folks what they wanted and the truth be damned).

Aboard the SS United States, in the echoing lounge and above in the breeze on deck, it was Beatle songs that we sang, all the songs that all of us knew, both Brits and Yanks in the lingo of the time.

We reached a truly great crescendo at this with the arrival at last of our sleek and stately ship after all those musical days and nights aboard.

Approaching New York Harbor and a glide past the Statue of Liberty, the ship's upper deck became swiftly packed with Hendra and Ullett fans, foremost among them David and me and the Painesville girls but also a makeshift choir of other passengers, all ready to serenade Lady Liberty with the Beatles' latest hit.

"Close your eyes and I'll kiss you," swooned this crowd. Ah, such a song!

"Tomorrow I'll miss you" we all crooned in unison, followed with a swell of volume under Hendra's direction, "Remember I'll always be true," and then, importantly "while I'm away I'll write home every day and," getting noisier now, with something of a yell, "I'll send all my loving to you!"

Blissed out by this whole storyline, I imagined that Liberty's head now turned toward us with a creak as she smiled at the finale: "I'll pretend that I am kissing, the lips I am missing ..."

It was then that my new pal David caught what I tried my best to hide from him, a tear wet my eye. Now I knew that he knew that kissing was as far as Mary and I had ever gone. Oh, God, I missed her so, I wanted her, my vicar's daughter. How wonderful it was, our kissing, on that magical evening in my parents' car, parked beside the monastery next door, the hooded monks gliding silently by us like ghosts on both sides of the car with all its windows misted up from our suppressed passion.

And so the time had come to say goodbye to the Painesville girls, each one of them by name, swearing we'd see them again just as soon as we'd gotten ourselves one of those bloated American cars and could set off on the open road.

Chapter 3

What we'd seen from the bow of the ship as she prepared to dock along the Hudson was the view into Manhattan's West Side, tempting, a touch of mayhem and hundreds of taxicabs.

But our first impression of New York City itself was overwhelming. A place of jackhammers and cranes, whole streets under reconstruction, the air thick with exhaust fumes, glass and steel soaring into the air. This was not the sleek American city such as Los Angeles we'd seen in the movies and on TV. This was a city devoted to the realization of its wildest dreams.

David and I spent our first nights in gaudy Gotham — I told him the name meant literally a place of goats and fools — at the YMCA in midtown. There we came across a dispiriting number of fellow Brits and Europeans whom we'd not come all this way to meet.

While at the Y we spent most of our time scouring employment ads in the newspapers, coming quickly to appreciate that our combined pocket money would run out sooner than anticipated. David was braver at the job hunt than me, prepared to use up fistfuls of coins on calls in response to ads for the unlikeliest of jobs. Something called a "swabber" at a Times Square peep-show theater, for example. Meanwhile I considered myself simply unemployable.

On our fourth day in town, David strode into the storefront office of Thomas Cook and came out hired as a travel agent.

By then I'd decided to do the even more daring thing. I telephoned my father in England, reversing the charge.

"Hey, Dad, New York is just wonderful, it's so alive. It's the place to be!"

"That's good, son," he said. "So what do you need?"

"I can't find a job."

"Oh, for God's sake." Dad was an attorney (called a solicitor in England) and he'd once visited the White House on some fancy legal junket to Washington.

"Call this number," he said.

I took a note of it and then called it right away.

"Conrad Hilton here," said a voice. "Ah," I said. Pause. "My dad said I should call you for a job."

"Oh for God's sake," he said. Pause. "But I like your accent. Report tomorrow at the Hilton at Central Park South. They're looking for an elevator operator. Tell them I sent you."

The next morning, they dressed me up like the King of the Belgians with shoulder epaulets and white gloves. Thereafter my elevator became my nightly home six days a week. Once more I encountered the Duchess of Windsor as well as any number of celebrities I couldn't quite place, selling them each a copy of next morning's New York Times delivered to me every night tied up in a bundle and each worth a fat tip on top of the cover price. My customers all loved the English accent except for a fellow employee from Ireland who once punched my car's express button for the top-floor penthouse and pummeled me with his fists all the way up until I tumbled from the car onto the carpet at the final stop. I never did get my own back, to the fury of David who threatened to come to the hotel and seek revenge. I told him I'd rather turn the other cheek.

There was just one important adaptation we found we had to make to fit into America's world of work and that was to use underarm deodorant, an unknown commodity in Britain at the time. We also quit smearing Brylcreem on our hair, a hair styling pomade that only what we called the "spivs," the smooth boys and slackers, used in the States. One other expense was the purchase of an all-important transistor radio plus endless batteries so we could tune in to 1010 WINS New York AM. And then, of course, we had the cost of our daily visit to Tad's for a steak and potato and Coca Cola, an unbelievable bargain at less than $2. The secret of a glass of Coke was its hit of cold fizz and dark sweetness. Nothing else like it in the world back then, it seemed.

After a mere few weeks of regular paychecks and semi-starvation, David and I had accumulated, amazingly to us, enough cash to afford a one-bedroom apartment at number 13, Thirteenth Street.

And back at the Y we had fallen in with two New York fellows who'd soon become the ones to steer us toward an affordable car and thus complete our American good fortune and independence.

Billy was tall, an athletic guy from Brooklyn, and Andy was short, a bespectacled character from the Bronx. They fell for our accents and desired to spend as much of their spare time, which was plentiful, in our company. It was they who introduced us to Times Square and to Greenwich Village, both places essentially of nightlife all day, where we'd discover Horn and Hardart, the automat for endless hanging out, and the women's prison with its walls of brick, anguished yells falling from above the Village streets.

They also took us to the West End Lounge, an uptown hangout of the beats across from Columbia University where black hipsters took immediate exception to our syncopated use of the word "man!" quite common back then in England but offensive to blacks when used by whites in the States.

And it was Billy and Andy who shared with us our first-ever puff of marijuana, standing right in the open on a neon-lit side street midtown. "Do these two remind you of Jack Kerouac and Allen Ginsberg?" I asked David.

"No idea," he said.

But it was they who would — oh man, yes! — put us on the road.

"Have we got a deal for you," announced Billy on that blinking, blazing Saturday on Broadway and Forty Second. "We need to unload something on you two." Andy added to the pitch. "You fine gentlemen have been chosen. No questions asked."

How could we refuse the offer? A 1957 Plymouth Savoy, almost new, complete with press-button automatic gears, tail wings big enough to stuff our luggage into, a metallic color job and semi-bald (not completely bald) tires.

"Call it $600 cash, right now," sang Kerouac and Ginsberg. The deal was finally consummated at a reconnoiter spot on Henry Street in Brooklyn Heights, right by the home of Norman Mailer whom I happened to know had not so long ago published an essay in the journal Dissent called "The White Negro."

Done. We were on our way.

Chapter 4

As both of us left work for the last time, we each found find ourselves gazing up Fifth Avenue to its farthest portal on the horizon, the blue of the early summer sky beckoning, tempting us to taste the rest of America that lay in wait.

Yet we were enraptured by the glitter of Times Square just one last time, lured into a scene that was always lying in wait: the women of 42nd Street with their bizarre stockings and the men whose eyes sparkled with glycerin.

And there were a couple more vital things that needed to be accomplished before, as Huck Finn put it, we lit out for the territories.

I insisted we attend the American premier of "A Hard Day's Night" in Times Square. Then David wanted to catch the Rolling Stones on their first visit to America, live at the Peppermint Lounge. I was a Beatles fan and, as it were, a good boy, and he was a Stones fan and a bad boy — characterizations subject to complete reversal as we continued to get to know each other. We'd already found out that I was the one completely out of control while he had it all together.

"A Hard Day's Night" was opening at a cinema in Times Square. By the time we got there we discovered, amazed, that it had attracted more boys than girls, many of them carrying guitars, which seemed a trifle laughable to us. We were lucky to get seats in a full house of young people all smoking cigarettes; it made for a memorable afternoon. But so did the movie: that hauntingly extended opening note and the shock that it was in black and white had us riveted from the start. The event turned out to be an exercise in communication between us. He nudged my elbow at the line, "love is more than just holding hands" and I nudged him back at "you're not the hurting kind." The script was beyond perfect. "How do you find America?" a reporter asks John. "Turn left at Greenland," he says.

John later says to Paul's dirty old grandpa: "You should have gone to America."

And here we were.

Meanwhile, among the Times Square audience, the boys on their guitars were in rigorous competition with the screaming girls. And then the heavenly calm Ringo on his multi-cigarette, canal-side stroll to the tune of "This Boy" all but silenced the house.

We left the theater transmogrified, elated and homesick — "When I'm home, everything seems to be right" — so we simply wandered aimlessly around Times Square and took in its bizarre fixtures, especially the Viking whose job in life was to stand tall on the sidewalk all night. We had a long chat with him.

The movie had set us a million miles away from the deeply suspect Murray the K on 1010 WINS New York whose "loveable mop tops" language gave us the creeps. So the first thing David did when we got back to the apartment we were about to vacate was to break out his guitar and begin to play. He was really good. Surprisingly good. And I sang along in my highest tenor. "Now that's good!" he said. That Dick Lester/Alun Owen movie seemed to have seeded the germ of an idea.

Next up were the Rolling Stones. Or the possibility of them at least. We'd heard on the dreaded 1010 WINS that the Stones were arriving on their first U.S. tour and supposedly they might even put in a quick appearance in Manhattan at the Peppermint Lounge.

Wild news, too huge for David to ignore and I really went along with him on this, even though my own taste in pop other than the Beatles and of course Connie Francis ("I Worry and Wonder") leaned toward the bespectacled Buddy Holly, ("goin' faster than a rollercoaster") and, too, those anthemic strings and choirs of Ray Charles ("I've made up my mind to live in memory."). David's tastes, on the other hand, seemed harder, louder, darker and richer. He seemed to favor house parties that featured fake fistfights among the guests.

But who could resist a glimpse of the notorious Stones, founded by Brian Jones, a native of my own hometown of Cheltenham, led by the university-trained Mick Jagger and dominated by the guitar genius and blues historian Keith Richards?

And so, on the afternoon of the band's supposed arrival in Manhattan, David and I marched ourselves in haste to the Peppermint Lounge located at 128 West 45th Street.

This would be especially cool, surely. Guys with long hair were a rarity at the time, even in New York. Yet as we descended the steps to the club's basement entrance, we took nervous note of a thinning crowd. Where were the Stones?

"They're not coming," muttered a surly voice from among puddles of discolored water accumulating from air-conditioners in the well of the basement-level entrance.

"Long live the Beatles," I murmured.

David was too pissed off to speak. Instead he reached out for the corner of a poster floating at his feet. "Souvenir!" he announced, shaking the drips off it. A black-and-white photo printed on yellow card showed the Rolling Stones lined up against a limousine.

"Check this out," said David, leading the way back up to the sidewalk. Then he pointed to Brian Jones in the line up. "You look just like him."

"Nah," I said.

"You do," he insisted. "Light brown hair. Bags under your eyes."

"Well look at Keith, then," I parried. "You're just like him. Black hair. Wasted."

"I do," he agreed. "You're right. We have a couple of dead ringers here."

And so, out of the disappointment of a lost afternoon was born our nefarious plan: First, let's cut out this photo from the poster and stick it on the back window of the Plymouth Savoy. Then, with some white shoe polish we'd just spied in the window of a Fifth Avenue shoe store, we could write in big letters: THE ROLLING STONES – LONDON TO LOS ANGELES along the side of the car.

"Why not, Thom One?" said David.

"Yeah, David Carpenter, why not?" said I.

Chapter 5

Now we really were on the road. David was at the wheel and punching the chrome button on the dash of the Plymouth to change gear, a priceless process for anyone who'd learned to drive in England on an Austin 7.

And now for the first time the two of us were actually quarreling.

"Of course we have to go to Niagara Falls!" I yell at him. "Are you insane? How can we not go to Niagara Falls?"

"Unless you want us to pluck apples in Iowa," he said back at me, "we have just enough cash to get us to my uncle's place in L.A., and that's it."

Gas could be had for 30 cents a gallon in some states, a pittance compared to what we'd pay for petrol in Britain, but I knew what he meant.

And I couldn't argue with how well he already drove on the right, as opposed to the left as in Britain. We'd both had practice at this by not stepping into traffic off the sidewalks of New York.

I quickly realized that David wanted to go

straight to Painesville in order to meet up with the girls as soon as possible, which would be quite soon given our current speed of 75 mph.

David increased the speed, blasting past the Falls exit. Perhaps he was beginning to believe we couldn't bear each other without the company of girls.

The brand-new Interstate system we were on, built to Eisenhower's specifications that its hills and corners could safely convey a convoy of intercontinental missiles at 60 mph., was something we'd been craving to experience ever since we learned to drive.

Even the signs were amazing and they were uniform throughout the nation. Our own land of champion speedsters such as Stirling Moss would never have anything to compare with it, forever condemned to loopy lanes and cobbled streets that we all drove like maniacs anyway.

It was not long, of course, before a black-and-white sedan in the far lane began to pace us, steadily drawing closer alongside for the driver to check out the scrawl along the shiny, aluminum-blue finish of our vehicle: THE ROLLING STONES: London to Los Angeles.

The cop brought down his front window on the

passenger side and mouthed what looked like the words, "You boys are coming with me!"

"Open the window!" I yelled at David, now fumbling with the knobs by his side, never having operated an electric car window in his life.

The breeze whistled in but David was not slowing. Instead he was mouthing in the cop's direction, "Excuse me?"

The officer blinked at this, then barked, "Follow me!" while swerving in front of us and leading the way to an exit.

Once we were off the highway, David managed to squeal to a halt just yards behind the sheriff on the side of a dusty road. He was definitely a sheriff, with a badge that said so and in the way he fingered the holsters of his twin revolvers.

"So you boys are the Rolling Stones?"

"Brian Jones," I bleated at him. "And this is Keith Richards."

"Now, Richard," drawled the sheriff, addressing David. "Where in hell did you learn how to drive?"

"He's Keith," I corrected, leaning forward.

"Listen boys," announced the sheriff, "my daughter is very taken with you Rolling Stones." And with the air of a hunter dragging home the day's prey, he added, "I'm thinkin' that you two boys are gonna have to come with me."

And so we did, following his black-and-white with its couple of sirens on the roof and searchlight on the driver-side rear-view mirror, kicking up a cloud of dust and obscuring any hope of knowing where we were or how, at this point, we might ever get out of here.

While David drove, I swiveled around to reach the back seat and rummage for David's guitar. "What if they ask us to sing?" I said.

"Then we'll sing," said David, "like we did on the boat."

"May I remind you that I don't know any Stones songs," I said.

"Nor does anyone else," said David. "They haven't begun their tour here and they don't even have a hit in the States yet."

"We'll have to sing Beatles songs," I said in desperation, groaning as I hauled the guitar case on the back seat over to the front. "Follow my lead."

It must have been about cocktail hour on this warm day in May when a small-town sheriff has shanghaied us and in about half an hour we'll be on, performing the Rolling Stones' first unofficial performance in the United States of America. A catastrophe, surely.

We arrived at a rather neat little farmyard by the side of a two-story house. Chickens clucked around the sheriff's vehicle while we parked our car by the side of a hayrick.

"Hey, Debby," yelled our captor. "Lookee see what I have here!" Debby appeared at the front door. "It's two of them Rolling Stones."

"Lordee, Walter, what have you done now?" she said. "Sally!" she called. "Come on down."

As David and I clambered out of the Plymouth, the teen daughter of the house arrived in the yard, hiding behind her mother.

It was all smiles from us as we sauntered up to introduce ourselves. Debby smiling too, but rather nervously, reading out loud the lettering on the side of the car, '"London to Los Angeles," while Sally came into view, essentially hysterical, shivering in anticipation.

Sheriff Walt then beckoned us to join him for refreshments inside, where we noticed Debby in the kitchen, making several calls on the wall phone.

Uh-oh. Show time.

The rest is really a blur. About 20 couples

began to arrive, many with children, the yard and driveway filling up before our eyes with enormous automobiles.

These folks obviously couldn't wait for the fun. We were introduced to everyone and by the time dusk began to fall, David and I were comfortably seated on the lower stoop of a stepped haystack that faced the front of the house.

Our audience was obviously pretty much pickled already, their kids racing about the place until everyone hushed a bit as David theatrically began to tune his guitar. "Better this than a speeding ticket, I guess," he muttered in my direction.

We started with "Till There Was You," not strictly a Beatles number since it came from "The Music Man" but it was one of the tracks on the most recent Beatles album and everyone seemed to know the words. It seemed to be just the song to bring to light whatever talents we might have had, mine for singing in counter-tenor, hitting the lingering high notes, and David's for sounding like an entire orchestra when strumming his guitar full tilt. My God, I thought as he started up, he's fantastic. He's doing a wall-of-sound thing. I realized then we might actually get away with this. The next song brought a round of applause right away with its opening notes: "Oh please..."

David had chosen to ramp things up with "I Want to Hold Your Hand," the one about "being your man."

I too got a little cocky at this point with the audience singing along, quite oblivious of whether they were listening to the work of the Beatles or the Stones.

I caught the eye of Sally as she laughed and clapped her hands right beside us on the hayrick. Brazenly I beckoned her to follow me as David launched into a strumming solo. I raced behind the hayrick and she followed and I held her hand like the song said and in the delirium of the moment I let my lips deftly touch hers for just a second, the prettiest young lady I'd kissed since Mary back in England.

She laughed and I laughed and I carelessly blurted, "Hi, I'm T —" but she interrupted: "I know who you are, Brian," and then I took her hand and we scampered right up the back of the hayrick to the very top and stood looking out over the heads of the audience that was staring back up at us.

"Let's go!" I yelled, taking her hand and at each leap on our flight to the ground, holding hands and catching each other's eye and then smiling and smiling deeply back, we floated together in literal flight down the steps of that hayrick, leaping with each beat of the song further into the air and I saw those eyes flash at me as I'd never seen a pair of eyes flash before, my old Astaire in synch with her young Rodgers as she sweetly laughed at the applause of her family and friends, so we danced and leapt our way down that stack, step by step, holding hands just like the song said, all the while laughing along with the applause, I knew then — all is true! — that my life had just met its moment.

Chapter 6

"I almost blew it," I confessed the next morning as David roared the car out of there. "I nearly told her my name! But she interrupted me."

His eyebrows shot up as the wheels spun.

"She said, 'I know who you are, Brian.'"

"Oh great, moaned David. "Now she thinks she's kissed a Rolling Stone."

"She was great," I said. "That ski-jump nose..."

"My type, too," said David. "Congratulations, Thom One. You made her look like an angel, dancing down the hay."

"And you sounded like Django Reinhardt!" I said. We were now speeding on toward Ohio and the Painesville girls.

Last night had changed everything. What we really wanted from the girls now, after what happened yesterday, was permission to proceed, to keep on singing for our supper.

The sheriff had let us sleep in the Plymouth parked in his yard overnight (no sleeping under the same roof as his daughter!). The plan was that we'd sleep in the car the whole way across the country so we could afford our daily ration of unfiltered Pall Mall cigarettes. This had been an excellent start.

But something else had happened since last night, too. We'd just heard it on the radio: "In an achievement unlikely ever to ever be equaled," went the news flash, "in the first the week of April 1964, The Beatles have occupied the top five positions with records from six record labels on each of the Hot-100 charts in the nation."

Our lads from Liverpool were now topping the charts with "Can't Buy Me Love," "Twist and Shout," "She Loves You," "I Want To Hold Your Hand," "Please Please Me," "I Saw Her Standing There," "From Me To You," "Do You Want To Know A Secret," "All My Loving," "You Can't Do That," "Roll Over Beethoven" and "Thank You Girl."

"Thank you, Beatles!" yelled David, slapping the rim of the steering wheel. I knew what he meant. The Rolling Stones had only had a measly four hits back in Britain: "Come On," "I Wanna Be Your Man," "Not Fade Away" and "It's All Over Now" but David and I knew none of them at all. And none of them were yet hits in the States.

While Beatlemania had already become an epidemic in America, David's and my favorite pop music still came from the likes of the Shangri-Las, so operatic and played constantly late at night over Radio Luxembourg, the station for U.S. troops in Europe. David's favorite group, he told me, was the Dave Clark Five, powder kegs of energy whose "Glad All Over" and other hits were already selling six million records a month back home.

Another pop star we both admitted fancying was Sandy Shaw, a British hit-maker and friend of the Beatles, rumored to be as shortsighted as John Lennon and with a gaze so intense it was intriguing. Her bare feet in her TV appearances were weirdly appealing, too.

During the miles that we were now covering at about 70 mph on impeccably virgin tarmac, we encountered many a hitchhiker, girls and boys both, and were tempted to give them rides if only as an audience for our performance rehearsals, but that would have meant having to unpack David's guitar and anyway we needed an empty car by the end of the day so we could park in some field and sleep. We had no fear of strangers or deserted fields because something was happening in the early 1960s and we felt we knew what it was. The only thing the least invasive that we had to fear, being visitors who were exempt from the draft for at least six months, were those old geezers remaining on the House Committee on Un-American Activities that had been demonized back in Britain for at least a decade.

The topics we discussed in the car at night were ones that would ultimately wrap us in silence and bring the release of sleep.

"You want to put Sandy Shaw's toes in your mouth," David would declare from the front seat while a stub of a Pall Mall smoldered in the front or the rear ashtray. "You're a foot fetishist."

"Oh for God's sake," I said.

"Let me remind you," he went on, "that my goal on this trip is to invade America and then deliver you from evil."

"Let me remind *you*," I said, "that true love comes from the suppression of sexual intercourse."

""Are you kidding?" he said. "Let me straighten you out about all this. America is still wild; they shoot their presidents here, OK. And it's in the wild that truth resides."

Mark Howell

"David, you and I are as different as JFK and LBJ, don't you see?"

And with that we'd sleep like kings.

Chapter 7

Soon came the time to forewarn the girls from the SS United States that we were about to arrive on our self-appointed visit.

After endless hours of driving across industrial Ohio, we'd reached the outskirts of Painesville and David was calling ahead from a phone booth and then announcing to me that it was my turn to drive so he could be personally greeted by their welcoming party.

And so he was, managing to remember all their names.

"Hello Shirley!" "Hello Paula!" "Hello Beverley!" "Hello Elaine!" "Hello Irene!" "Hello Kathleen!" "Hello Gail!" "Hello Donna! "Hello Lois!" "Hello Darlene!"

This is how it went.

Both David and I had been as nervous as naked boys because we'd been waiting for what was about to happen for weeks. Now here they were, within touching distance once more. A lot of fantasizing had gone on before this moment.

Forewarned and possibly forearmed, all 20 of them had assembled in the courtyard of Lake Erie College awaiting our arrival. And here now in this noble space with its sweeping driveway in front of a massive, multi-windowed pile of red brick, when the girls caught sight of those words about the Rolling Stones from London to Los Angeles, they actually screamed.

Beverley broke from the crowd and skipped toward us. "You're going to have to park this, OK? Over there, by the side? We'll come rescue you."

So David slunk the car around the corner to abandon it by what he called "these dustbins." "Garbage cans," I corrected him.

Beverly and Gail were the first to catch up with us, each of them a blast of springtime in their pleated skirts and white socks. We didn't even have any short pants, never brought any from England where such things were not required attire at any time or place except for schoolboys.

The girls shuffled us into the building and along a corridor to some sort of common room. "So you're really doing the singing thing?" said a glaring Gail, her tone a mix of awe and despair. She had been my personal favorite back on the boat and I'd been forever smiling at her. "You have a lovely voice," she'd whispered as the Statue of Liberty finally slid by us to the sound of the Beatles serenade.

Beverly, who'd taken a blatant shine to David on the voyage, was now being quite as bossy as I remembered her back then and insisted he get his guitar from the car so she and Paula and several of the others too could join us in a sing-along.

It actually turned out wonderfully well. Once again I hadn't really anticipated that the two of us, along with everyone joining in, could do the Beatles so spot on that even the Stones were swept to oblivion. Nobody wanted to hear the Stones anyway, not here in Ohio, not yet.

Not that either David or I were up on the Stones, either. We didn't have a clue what "Little Red Rooster" meant, other than something unmentionable.

We sang the five songs from "A Hard Day's Night" that we'd been rehearsing in the car across the endless spaces of Ohio. It was with sweet relief we realized that several of the girls knew some Beatles lyrics as well and joined in. The rapturous applause after each number was as much for themselves as for us. I joined in the clapping myself because once again, David had acquitted himself so marvelously.

Then Lois had her say: "I'm glad you don't have their hair," she declared. The others nodded vigorously. The U.S. press along with most of its readers were already fixated on the Beatles haircuts and the long hair of the rest of the British bands, one teen magazine quoting Eric Burdon calling his band "a bunch of animals really."

Our noisy little concert soon devolved with the crowd scattering into various directions until finally I was left chatting with Gail while David wandered off with Beverly.

As so often happens when a fellow shares his thoughts with a girl, both their thoughts ultimately wander their way toward another guy or another girl. So it was with Gail who determined that she needed to know more about "your girl back home."

I melted immediately and spilled the story, how my vicar's daughter had cried when I left for Southampton and the far side of the Atlantic and who was still in my heart. She was just 18 now and I really did wish she were here with us on this trip, although I knew that was just crazy.

"Is she a Stones fan?" Gail asked

"No, no," I said. "She's all 'Twist and Shout.'

We do the twist till we're drenched."

"So do you want to call Mary and tell her how you feel?"

It was a provocative idea but one I'd been quite unable to come up with myself, an overseas phone line being beyond my reach at this point in our travels.

"We have access to an overseas line right here that's billed to our parents," she said. My mom wouldn't mind if I made a call like that."

"She wouldn't?"

"She's divorced. She's rich."

At this news and my first-ever encounter with a child of divorce, I stumbled and mumbled for a moment. Then I seized it. Let's do it," I said.

Next thing I'm standing in a narrow booth of steel and tinted glass with Gail squeezed in beside me. I began talking to an operator. In a short while I overheard a British accent, then some clicks and clacks and then I heard, as though through the mouth of an endless tunnel, the muffled sound of Mary's voice, half a world away in Gloucestershire in the west of England. She'd answered the phone herself. It must have been nine at night over there and her parents were probably snoozing already.

"Hello, this is Mary,"
"Oh wow," I gasped. "This is Thom."
"Who?"
"Thom One, Mary. It's me."
We clicked at last and our minds came together.
"Where are you?" she asked. "How can you be calling?"
A moment of guilt seized my throat. "There's someone here who's lent me her phone. We're at a school near Cleveland."
"It's amazing to hear your voice," she said, seeming to be as distant and as close as the wind.
"Wonderful to hear yours," I said. "I love you Mary."
A pause.
Pregnant, it occurred to me, would be the unlikely adjective.
"Listen," she said. I have some news."
Dread might be the right word now.
"Thank you for all your letters," she went on. "They're wonderful."
That feels better.
"So I showed them to Lawrence Durrell."
Whoa!
"Mum and dad took me to Corfu with them on

holiday. We met Mr. Durrell for dinner at a friend of Dad's."

"What did he say?" I asked.

"Hello?"

"I mean about the letters!"

"Well, he was very polite," she said.

"Polite?"

"He said your writing was sub-Kerouac."

"Kerouac? — He said *Kerouac*?" I yelled, my heart taking off like a bird. Lawrence Durrell had compared me to Kerouac! Oh my God. *My God*! This was probably the biggest thing to have happened to me in all my life.

"Mary, I love you."

"I love you!" she said.

That's next best thing I'd heard in my life.

When we were back in the car, later that day, as David and I headed west in our own adventure on the road, David was incredulous. "You called Mary?"

"Yes, and Lawrence Durrell compared my writing to Kerouac."

"You called Mary?"

"She said she loves me."

"Well, well, well," repeated David.

The thing about Kerouac, I told him, was this:

He once wrote a golden utterance as useful to me as Whitman's "Song of the Open Road." He said, "I saw my life was a vast glowing empty page and I could do anything I wanted."

To explain this to David, still stuck on the news about Mary, I'd have to tell him about my experience of Samadhi one lovely afternoon while taking a walk, a rare moment with the family dog but without my brother, at a place called Leckhampton Hill in the Cotswolds that overlooked the town of Cheltenham — known as Queen of the Cotswolds — gazing at a view so glorious that my heart and my mind expanded as if I'd just been reborn into a world I'd already come from. I must have been 16 at the time and ever since that inexpressible freedom I'd become a manic hoarder of vagabond reflections, a collection so endless it threatened to overwhelm me with boxes of papers packed to the brim with the scribbles and scrawls of my wilder friends.

David, silent at the wheel, finally said that all he knew about Kerouac was that the King of the Beats had never really done a day's work in his life.

Chapter 8

Life goes on and by now we're almost half way across the United States. Not the old Route 66 way but the faster, new Interstate way. No stopping us now.

We'd probably consumed about a hundred packs of unfiltered Pall Malls by now and spent many, many nights in the Plymouth Savoy, the pattern of its seat covers, front and back, engraved on our cheeks.

We'd washed up in countless gas-station men's rooms and we'd let our hair grow long and had discussed the nature of life and the universe and of women.

And we had performed Beatle songs at the invitation of at least 15 American households, invited into their homes for an afternoon delight on account of that slogan still plastered on the side of the Plymouth, largely catching the eye of women whose cars were parked in the same tight little supermarket lots where we'd stopped to stock up on cigarettes. These were women who would usually be at home during the day. Their kids, fresh out of school, would know who the Rolling Stones were. And we were fed well for our services, which were getting better and better all the time.

How many housewives and their offspring still believe that back in the summer of 1964 they and the kids were serenaded by two of the Rolling Stones?

The righteousness of this would, we were sure, one day come to vex us. But the situation at the time was both simple and complicated.

We had to eat and we wanted to sing, the minstrel's equation: that seemed simple. But larks and legends, the raw material of rock 'n roll, were as true as you wanted them to be. David was forever telling me the same thing he told our hosts whenever they declared that they could not believe two of the Rolling Stones were singing Beatles songs in their house: "It's only true in reality," whatever that meant, but it did seem to work.

But not necessarily for David or me. The biggest media moment we'd experienced in our lives was Walter Cronkite announcing that the president of the United States had been shot and was dead. What if *he* was making it all up? What would that mean?

Don't ask, we said. This was the Sixties.

We're not in Kansas anymore.

As a matter of fact it was in Kansas that something happened we wished we could undo, that we prayed was not true in any reality.

The new highway that appeared to run directly east to west across the whole state of Kansas was paralleled by a transcontinental railroad. This would provide us with a distraction as we traveled. Whenever we flashed our headlights at the oncoming locomotive, its engineer would keep blasting his horn as he slammed by us. It was great, noisy fun.

Until one afternoon a pink convertible roared up behind our car and accelerated past us at great speed, just as we flashed our lights at an oncoming, super-long freight train going at its own high speed across the prairie. The pink convertible's driver was a young blonde woman whose hair streamed behind her as she raced by, not even looking at us. Then, when we flashed our lights at the train, its engineer responded with an endless blast of his own, one that continued as the freight cars roared by.

The blonde in the convertible, now well ahead of our car, seemed to jerk her steering wheel slightly as the train's horn filled the air, sending her car into a swerve that she was immediately unable to control. The roar and the clatter of the train filled our ears while we watched in horror as the woman at the wheel swerved wildly from one lane to another until her convertible tipped and then rolled over and kept rolling over as it scattered debris across the highway.

David screeched us to a stop, just avoiding a collision with the wreck. The train churned on, its driver oblivious of the disaster and unaware of whether his horn — which I guess we had provoked — was to blame for distracting the driver's attention.

I piled out of our car and ran to the one that now lay upside down but could see no sign of the woman. By this time David too was soon out of the Plymouth, and several other vehicles traveling in both directions had come to sudden stops amid the trail of debris. Like a movie in hellish slow motion I was riveted by the mess, a tangle of twisted metal, a stream of plastic lipstick tubes, combs, hairbrushes and scattered clothing.

I fell to my knees beside the upturned car,

peering to see if she might be trapped beneath and to pray for her if she was.

I was shaking convulsively when David came up behind me. "It's alright, Thom," he murmured, his hand on my shoulder. "She's not under there. She's likely been thrown off the road. Come back to the car." I was sobbing by now.

David had to hold me upright when we reached the Plymouth.

"I'll make this up to you," he said to me, so seriously. "You're a man of faith and you don't deserve all this hell."

Chapter 9

We never did see her body by the time the ambulance arrived. And we'd accelerated out of there at the first wail of the police sirens with no idea what else to do. This was to be our one and only blink into the merciless maw of the modern world's motorway.

Meanwhile back in the west of England, half a world away, my girl Mary was missing me while I missed her, madly. And told David so, at the risk of hearing one more time that such pining was unmanly and exposed my lack of sexual experience.

"Ever seen her naked?" he'd taunt, summoning up uncontrollable images partly divine but mostly, bafflingly, profane.

However important this all might be, we now faced some practical choices that needed to be made. Our ultimate decisions would be radical:

Yes to Pike's Peak in Colorado.
No to the Grand Canyon in Arizona.
Yes to Bryce Canyon in Utah.

No to Las Vegas in Nevada.

The last was the easiest one. We didn't have the kind of money that we could lose a bunch of it in Vegas.

"And," added David, "the Grand Canyon is just a hole in the ground."

"That's 14 miles long," I said wistfully.

So Pike's Peak and Bryce Canyon it was. The peak turned out to be a literal high point, naturally. Fourteen thousand feet up, one of 50 or so peaks in Colorado that reached that height, this one was named, we discovered, after a fellow named Zebulon Pike, Jr. Its Arapaho name, we also found out, was Heey-otoyoo.

And Bryce Canyon turned out to be beyond belief, hundreds of thousands of little pink towers called hoodoos poking up out of the Paunsaugunt Plateau like nothing we'd ever seen or even imagined. All we'd tell our pals back home would be, "Go there."

Now we were free at last to head north to Wyoming so we could also tell those pals that we'd seen with our own bare eyes the magically named townships of Cheyenne and Laramie. Magical mainly because "Laramie" was the American TV series shown on BBC in Britain featuring those two ranch partners who ran a stagecoach operation. Not necessarily a favorite of Mary's but everyone else would be speechless to learn that we'd actually been to such mythical cities.

But first a revelation on exactly why it was that David mostly had the wheel of the car rather than me. Here's how that went.

While in the outer reaches of Denver, we decided to attend, for the first time in our lives, a phenomenon we'd vaguely heard of known as a drive-in movie. Nothing else like it in the whole wide world, this would be a concept that had cruelly tempted us for its unlikeliness and its wild promise, much like a striptease, whatever that might be.

Showing in a nearby suburb was a newly released film called "Dr. Strangelove: Or How I Learned to Love the Bomb," by Stanley Kubrick, whose dark humor we knew would stick with us for the rest of our lives. Such lines: "Gentlemen, please — you can't fight in here, this is the War Room!"

Sitting side by side on the wide front seat of the Plymouth with me behind the wheel, we became so gobsmacked by the movie that neither of us paid much attention when I eventually reversed out of there and took off for the exit. It was a maneuver that quickly cracked the passenger window in two while the speaker, formerly attached to the top of that window, now flopped wanly off its post.

The window was a goner. So was the theater's speaker. Oh, the horror!

We shamefully hightailed it out of there and about a mile down the road in the darkness, David told me to pull over, which is when I made things worse. With the jack from the trunk, I struck the damaged window twice in an effort to remove the remaining glass. What happened instead was that two splintery holes appeared in the window looking exactly like two fresh bullet holes.

Oh dear.

And so it was that on the road to Cheyenne and Laramie we were pulled over by a Wyoming motorcycle cop who aimed his gun at us and yelled a question about what the hell kind of fight we'd been in.

No answer from us.

"You boys are coming with me!" was what we heard one more time.

Chapter 10

Amazingly, the morning of our one-hundredth day heading west across the United States was the very first time that Brian Jones and Keith Richards got to sleep in.

And our sincere thanks for this ultimately had to go to the cop escorting us on behalf of the highway patrol of Wyoming to police headquarters due to those two unexplained bullet holes piercing our passenger-side front window. He'd paid no mind to the lettering alongside the car proclaiming us famous rock stars but he did try to tell his station sergeant that the holes were the result of reversing out of a drive-in movie theater. "The hell they are," said the sergeant.

"But we're the Rolling Stones," said David, which was his chosen explanation.

"The hell you are," repeated the sergeant.

The rest of that day went to getting at the truth and the lie both. The whole tangle was somewhat disappointing for a couple of limeys (the sergeant's words) who'd been raised on Broderick

Crawford as the hero of "Highway Patrol," still a big hit on British TV.

The situation finally landed on four wheels once the police chief asked us for a song. "Right here, right now," he said. We gave him "Eight Days a Week," a new hit for the Beatles. David put on a stirring performance as Mr. Richards on acoustic guitar and I achieved new peaks in counter-tenor falsetto as Mr. Jones, these efforts fueled by our sheer amazement at how much wilder even than anticipated this Laramie leg of our British invasion was becoming.

The chief loved it all and instructed his staff to let us park in the station's yard overnight, then kindly proffered the address of a repair shop close by that might give us a deal on a window replacement.

So we slept deeply, right through the 4 a.m. shift change, and didn't get to leave the place until almost noon, which was the when the chief, back for his shift, gave us a spirited wave as both a Stones and a Beatles fan.

The west then went wilder still, indeed it was about to change our lives forever, just as we tooled along Main Street on our way to the repair shop as instructed. A rusting pick-up truck overtook us at a leisurely rate so the driver and the passenger could check out the sign on the side of our car.

Once they were past us we got to check out their silhouettes through the grubby rear window of their truck.

They had long, dark hair topped by great white Stetsons.

"Cowgirls!" yelled David. "The chase is on!"

He nudged us ever closer to their truck's rear end. Both girls looked around at us. Dark skin. Rich black hair. Just lovely. David backed us off somewhat so I could smile and wave at them. But they speeded up. Then the address of the repair shop came up fast and too soon we had to turn into its forecourt. "Oh, lamentable loss," I said.

A mechanic wandered up, took a careless look at the bullet holes and told us what the repair would cost us (a lowball estimate thanks to a call from the police chief). And then, stunningly, came the return of the Stetson girls in the pickup.

We watched them as they sashayed their way toward us in those epically huge hats and we took note that they were, in fact, suppressing their laughter, having done a wild U-turn to come back and take a closer look at these Rolling Stones.

We stared right back at them. And right then,

somewhere deep inside, something told us that great good fortune was underway here, a silent wheeling in our journey. There was no way that any of us could have known it, but we were all now on cue for a naked girl in a tree house.

Could such a thing be possible?

Chapter 11

Their smiles were as wide as —yes— the rims of their hats. They were so super-cool, both of them, that we actually backed away, pretending to pay attention instead to the mechanic as he set out to replace our busted window.

"Hi," said the taller of the two.

"Hi yourself," said David.

"What kinda car is this?" she yelled at the mechanic, banging away with his tools.

"Plymouth," he said, stuck on his knees.

"So you pilgrims are from Massachusetts," she said to David.

"My name's David, David Carpenter," he said. "And this is Thom, Thom One. We're pilgrims from England."

"I'm Winona," said the shorter of the two. "And this is Hedi. It means 'I know.' My name means first-born daughter. We're Lakota."

Tossing aside their hats, they lounged on the beat-up couch just next to the scene of our repair. We stared at then. They were hauntingly good-looking and we found ourselves at a loss for words.

"Let's go for a ride, guys," said Hedi. "Your car's not near ready."

Before we knew it we were squeezed between them on the front seat in their truck, Hedi at the wheel. We silently agreed to let Hedi take us on a spin to nowhere.

"What's this?" said David, fingering a bundle of feathers dangling from the rear-view mirror. "It's a dream catcher," said Winona. "You never seen one of them?"

"The plains are filled with dreams," explained Hedi. "Good dreams and bad. The good ones pass through the ring, the bad ones get caught in the web." Already she was the Hedi of my dreams. "You're a good one," I told her, looking her in the eye but barely able to hold it.

At that exact moment another pickup came barreling past us and I saw three guys and the driver grinning at us. Sickly grins. I could tell David caught those grins too.

It was in such moments among strangers when we communicated by looks that we felt most like two of the Rolling Stones.

Strangely, though, the topic of the Stones

never came up on that trip in Hedi's truck, kind of a heavenly relief. When we got back to the repair shop, we left the two of them in the idling truck while we paid for the new front-side window (the equivalent of a week's tips as an elevator operator in a Fifth Avenue hotel).

Before we left on our own from the shop, I leaned against Hedi's window and said I'd like to see her again, truly the most forward thing I'd done since making that overseas call to Mary. Meanwhile, at the other window, David appeared to be chatting up Winona. Delicious. Who knew what might come of it?

We'd find that out soon enough. Later in the day, in early evening, we were cruising Laramie's Main Street along with every other young driver in town on a Saturday night. And frankly we were hoping to run into Winona the eldest born and Hedi who knows it all.

Instead we were run into ourselves. It was just a tap from behind at first, a slight engagement with our rear bumper at a red light from the vehicle behind us. But before the light changed, we felt our car being pushed ahead into cross traffic. David stood on the brake while I opened the passenger door to yell at the idiot behind. I recognized the guy who'd sneered at us during our drive with Hedi and Winona. Now he bumped us so hard the Plymouth took an involuntary leap ahead and David got ready to step out himself and confront the guy.

Even as he unlatched his door, the car behind squealed into a curve around us and from out of my window I heard him spit the sibilant words that would now guide our lives.

"You son of a Sioux!"

Chapter 12

That car overtaking us kept bristling with insults, mainly from the driver whose eye caught mine as he flashed by within touching distance of my open window.

David at the wheel took chase until I spat, "Stop it!"

"What's the matter, Thom One?" he said, pulling back a bit. "Scared of some action?"

"I don't see how someone else's problem is our problem," I mumbled.

"What kind of priest would you make, huh?" he said. He was truly pissed off now. "What do you want to do with your holy soul, roll around in heaven all day like the Beatles?"

That youths' car had now outraced us so the crisis was presumably over for now.

"What do *you* want to do?" I yelled at him. "Piss against garage walls like the Stones?"

I obviously wanted to get my own back and I wanted to explain myself. "I truly believe," I said ludicrously, "that a person should pay rent just once in their life and never have to again. I believe that one razor should last a lifetime. I believe people should solve their own problems and not ask me."

Which made everything much worse.

"Oh my God," swore David, "you are so unbelievably entitled. Have you ever done anything worthwhile in your life?"

"I helped buy this car from my elevator job," I reminded him.

"So you had your ups and downs," he said.

Then I saw them. Hedi and Winona, both with their Stetsons pulled back, standing on the sidewalk, signaling to us to stop, their truck parked a little ahead of them. David pulled over behind their pickup and we jumped out to join them. I pecked Hedi on the cheek. David kissed Winona on the lips.

"We know those boys," they said.

Steer clear of them, they're garbage," warned Winona.

"They're idiots, Win, they can't help it," said Hedi.

Then, out of the blue, "Would you sing to us please?" they pleaded.

"'Sure we will," said David, so promptly I gave

him a sharp look. And sharper still when Win added: "but first a test."

Uh oh.

"What do you mean, a test?" I said. I was lousy at tests.

"Win just found this teen magazine with biographies of each of the Rolling Stones."

Uh-oh indeed. So while we sat trapped between the girls on the seat of their pickup, Win would grill us both with questions derived from some ballsy little rag that pretended it had an in with Jagger and the boys.

"So, Brian, you first, OK?" said Win. I gulped. "Yeah, go right ahead."

"How old are you and where were you born?"

"I am 22 and I was born in Cheltenham." That was easy for me, having been born there myself and heir already to a whole passel of first-hand stories about Mr. Jones. "I once borrowed a Jaguar XK for a test drive from the Jag salesroom," I disclosed, "and "and crashed it on Landsdown crescent, went through a shop window in fact. My dad had to bail me out." All is true, but as Hedi was flashing me a startled gaze at such revelations, I reminded her that that her name meant "she knows." "So now you do."

"Next question," said Win. "What's your middle name?"

Uh oh. A pause.

"Hopkin," I hazarded.

"Correct!" she yelled and Hedi actually screamed.

"How many cigarettes do you smoke a day?"

"Sixty a day," I said. "Woodbines unfiltered. They're cheap.

"You are correct, of course!" said Win.

"Next. What jobs did you have before you started up the Rolling Stones?"

"I was a lorry driver."

"What's a lorry?" she asked.

"It's a truck," said Hedi and I gazed at her with pride.

"Now it's Keith's turn," said Win. "This is fun."

"Wait a minute," he said, let's see this fan magazine of yours." Win handed over a glossy but much thumbed publication that declared it the work of Andrew Loog Oldham, whom we both recognized as the first manager of the Rolling Stones from the early Crawdaddy Club days in Richmond, a fellow of whom we were admittedly quite jealous, along with a lot of other free-wheeling young men in England at the time.

"Are you ready?" said Win. I crossed my fingers on David's behalf as he nodded his assent.

"Where and when were you born?"

"In Dartford, Kent, in 1943," said David.

"Bingo," said Win.

"Was your family musical?

"Nah," said David. "My dad hates rock 'n roll and wouldn't have it in the house."

"Wait a minute," said Win. "It says here your grandfather had a band." I froze.

"That was my mother's dad. He was a jazz freak, famous too. My mom bought me my first guitar, which I still play."

"Quite right," said Win. This was spectacular from David. But he wasn't done.

"If you must know, I once sang in a trio of boy sopranos at Westminster Abbey in front of the Queen."

"That's what it says here!" said Win. I too was overjoyed, having had no idea about that side of Keith.

"You really are who you say you are, aren't you?" exulted Hedi.

David looked at me and I looked at him and this innocent remark was all we needed to justify our impersonation of famous strangers to strangers. We were meant to give it a try, no question about it.

"Come on, you two," said the girls in unison. "Sing to us!"

"Let's do it," said David. I nodded.

"We'll follow you," he said to Hedi.

And straight away we were a two-vehicle convoy headed down a narrow alley off Main Street in the very heart of Laramie. Now we could have some fun.

Within seconds we found ourselves in a gravelly, abandoned lot, the dead end of just the kind of strange alleyway, reeking and resonant with holy promise that Kerouac would dig. "How did you find this place?" I asked Hedi.

"We used to come here after school," she said. "Those boys did, too. They never hated Indians back then."

"Yes they did," said Winona.

"Well, you have to find your people," said Hedi."

Now David and his guitar were positioned on the front end of their pickup and we gathered as a tight little group up for the enjoyment of some, what? Pop n' roll?

"Ladies and ladies," I announced, presenting

the Rolling Stones!" at which we broke into "Can't Buy Me Love" by the Beatles, followed by "I Feel Fine," both big hits in a great year for songwriters John and Paul. Then my own sweet favorite, "If I Fell" with its subdued harmony for two at which David and I honestly excelled.

Then, just as we took a breath for our encore there came the noise of aggressive acceleration roaring up the alleyway and the snout appeared of a '64 Chevy Impala, "car of the year" carrying the three boys who'd bumped our ass on Main Street. One of them must be taking his daddy's new car for a spin.

Chapter 13

"I don't want this," I wailed to David. "We don't need it – it's none of our business."

"Oh for Christ's sake, Thom One," he barked. "Grow up!"

I was on the edge of tears but David had both fists balled up already. For a moment I thought he was going to hit me but then he jumped out of the car, just as the Impala skidded to a stop in a flurry of gravel and both its doors were flung open.

"You pair of Sioux suckers!" yelled the driver.

My eyes were open but my mind went black. I still couldn't believe what was happening. Even now I have no memory of getting out of the car or even of grappling with the door. All I now know is that my face was up against this punk's face, same height as me, surely the same age as me, same mad look in his eyes. And bam!

The sound was actually more of a crack as my fist landed right on his upper lip.

He yelled and I inhaled. My fist stung and it throbbed. His mouth spouted blood.

I launched into a yelling match with the other punk while Hedi and Winona leaped out of the Plymouth's back seat and really made noise. The alley echoed with it.

Without knowing what exactly it was doing, my right arm swung back once more and my brain went black again. Hedi had her arms around me, holding my upper body from behind and screaming so loud it left my right ear deaf.

Then she pulled me back so my spine went the wrong way and I watched while our two former adversaries scrambled back into their Chevy, then squealed into a reverse-gear retreat followed by the clatter of metal.

"They hit a dustbin!" yelled David gleefully.

"Trash can," I corrected.

Hedi swiveled me around and violently kissed me on the mouth, her lips and tongue exploring mine. Many seconds of bliss. No more pain in my fist.

The unbeatable high point so far in our journey across America.

Chapter 14

I was alone with Hedi in the Plymouth. David had gone off with Winona in their pickup.

"Did I ever tell you you're my hero?" asked Hedi one more time.

"Yeah you did," I said.

"Your hand feels OK?"

"No. I won't want to try that again. There are teeth marks on my knuckles."

"You won't have to do that again," she said. "You've already earned your ticket to heaven."

"You believe in heaven?" I asked. "You're Lakota."

"My dad is Lakota. My mom's from Poland."

"So you're part Indian," I said.

"I'm not part anything. I'm double."

"You are so cool," I said. "I am so glad I met you."

"I'm glad I met you," she said. But you're really too nice to be one of the Rolling Stones. Really."

"I punched that idiot in the mouth."

"The Stones are Satanic," she persisted.

"So you believe in Satan?"

"We live in evil times, Brian Jones. Our Vice President just shot the President, remember?"

I swerved to the curb, pulled on the hand brake and gazed at her. "It was Oswald who shot Kennedy," I said.

"You can't see that LBJ set it up?" she said. "We're all in hell now, you better believe it."

"Heaven and hell from you now, huh?"

It was precisely then, in the empty air that followed my meaningless remark, that she broke the silence with a deal no one could resist, angel or demon.

It took a while for me to absorb it but I was totally committed by the time I was ready to share it with David. With Keith Richards that is.

"Hedi has this uncle on her mother's side," I said, somewhat breathlessly, "who's built a tree house on a hillside in Marin County, which is north of San Francisco Bay in the State of California."

"Yes," he said.

"And he lets Hedi stay there whenever she wants."

"OK."

"And she wants to now. And she wants me to join her in a couple of weeks' time because I stood up for her in that stupid fight."

"Well, well."

"And whenever she stays there, she says, she's always naked,"

"Whoa!" yelled David. "You gotta count me in on this! Don't abandon me now, my brother!"

And so it was. We told Hedi we'd be at her tree house within the next couple of weeks. A leisurely straight shot from Laramie, we reckoned, through Salt Lake City, Reno, Sacramento, then finally and at last to Marin. We'd even get to go across the Golden Gate Bridge and not miss out on one of the great sights like we had with the Niagara Falls.

"Just take it easy on the road, you guys," said Hedi. "There's no rush."

"Oh, you have no idea," said David.

So within just a few days, equipped with a tangle of telephone numbers and addresses from Hedi and after a long, sad, loving goodbye with Winona, we were ready at last to set out on what might be the last lap of our Rolling Stones trip across the United States of America. Ready, that is, except for a couple of phone calls that David suddenly said he had to make, long-distance phone calls yet. We'd actually never made any phone calls after the one to Mary, let alone overseas. "You're not begging your parents for money, are you?" I asked. "It's a bit late for that and I don't think we really need it. We still have enough for petrol and cigs." And we'd each brought with us the air tickets back to London.

"Just some private business," he said. That hadn't come up before from either of us.

But we did see eye-to-eye right away on our renewed pledge to stick to a pair of cardinal rules: Never to do anything that the Beatles wouldn't do and don't do anything that the Stones wouldn't do.

Thus we set out on that long haul of geography through endless stretches of the wild and deserted and salty west, into and out of Utah, and then up toward the Montezuma Hills and finally into northern California with its detectable hint of heaven.

Pure anticipation had seemed to speed up the passage of time and space, melting days into nights, sun into moon, nightmares of blacktop into sweet dreams of the waves we'd surely surf on the coast. Like crusaders we fought our way over Battle Mountain and on toward the plush warmth of inland California.

From Oakley to Berkeley we talked as always about the subject that haunted us every moment. Were we deceiving the good people who so enjoyed being serenaded by two of the Rolling Stones?

"We're only deceiving ourselves," decided David, with bravura cunning, and I bought into that.

"It's all a laugh, isn't it, blameless and harmless," I said, "for them and for us, right? Where's the harm in it?"

It was in Berkeley, finally, that we made our only daytime stop as tourists. I was fascinated by this university town that I'd so much rather attend than either Oxford or Cambridge. David, meanwhile, anticipated eyeballing the host of co-eds swarming the streets.

We were not disappointed on Euclid Avenue at dusk. The atmosphere along this strip was positively Mediterranean with its open-air cafés and amazingly beautiful young people. The place made me think of Mary and I was suddenly overwhelmed by a crashing wave of guilt. And about time, too. What had I been thinking, flirting so outrageously with Hedi? What was I doing racing to enjoy her in the nude?

"I want to attend Berkeley with Mary," I blurted. This was too much for David and he made light of it immediately and disgracefully, coming to the conclusion that, "You're definitely not going to heaven, Thom One."

"Don't be so sure, David Carpenter, and I expect to see you there."

"I'm in heaven right now," he said, gazing around at the midday scene. "What could be finer than this?"

I was about to make a joke about the moon in Carolina but saw just in time an opportunity for David to say something profane and thought better of it.

Dusk was not far off and it was time to make haste to the treehouse over in Marin, however confused and two-minded I felt. Across the great Golden Gate we quickly encountered the woodlands of Marin with their golden oaks and mountain mahogany. It was stunning country and soon we found ourselves spending agonizing time in roadside phone booths trying to contact Hedi's uncle or Hedi herself.

Eventually we connected with them both but to me, all of a sudden, there seemed something amiss. Hedi had told us the location of the treehouse precisely to a fault but now she said she'd have to meet us nearby and walk us in. For his part, David seemed to be tolerating all these sudden twists and turns and finally we did indeed have exact directions and a proposed time of arrival.

Chapter 15

Then it was David who started acting strange. He insisted I get out of the car on the gravel drive that led to the treehouse and told me to go ahead and scope it out alone.

I got out of the car, looked back at him through the windshield and shrugged my shoulders.

He leaned out of the window and said, "Go ahead. Go up the ladder. Go on."

How odd of David to let me take the lead.

A premonition struck me that "life was but a dream if only we'd let it be." The phrase struck strangely home as I reached the ladder. So I began to climb the bamboo rungs when I heard, soaring through the open door above me, the chiming words of the loveliest song. I stopped climbing and took off my shirt and let it drop.

I heard a young woman's voice in song.

Looking back at David, I caught him waving his hand that I should keep going.

"Whenever we kiss" sang the voice, "I worry

and wonder."

Worry and I wonder. Whose voice is that?

It sang on like the wind with its own mysterious question "Your lips may be near but where is your heart?"

The voice spoke the words now. "It's always like this," it fretted, "I worry and I wonder."

"So do I," I whispered as I neared the top rung.

"You're close to me now," whispered the voice. And then the sound of a sigh. Almost a cry. "But where is your heart?"

My voice immediately, dangerously, precisely joined hers.

"We must break the spell," we sang together. "Won't you tell, darling, where is your heart?"

I clambered to the top, gasping in disbelief. My body flew into the treehouse, diving through the doorway and into its depths.

There stood, dear God, stark and naked, my Mary.

We stood face to face while she smiled and I placed my cool palms on her warm, smooth, skin, and stroked her flowing blonde hair and we kissed.

Gently, then deeply until our staring eyes closed completely.

Then softly once more as she sang again.

"Are you pretending I'm someone else?"

"Won't you tell me, darling, where is your heart?"

"I love you," I said. "I love you."

"I love you," she said.

All in a rush, she told me that David and Hedi had paid for her airfare from England and back because, miracle of miracles, they "owed you."

"They do?"

"David said he'd make it up to you when you saw a woman killed on the road. And Hedi said you put your own life in danger when protecting hers."

She whispered then to me, "I'm singing 'Where Is Your Heart?' because Connie Francis was our favorite singer and that was our favorite song. Do you remember?"

God bless her, I do. So beautiful, so sweet and not a stitch on.

This is the page that awaits the movie.

Chapter 16

"But who are you really?" she asked, squatting across from me on the treehouse floor. She wore shorts and a shirt and I my jeans and my only T-shirt.

"Who do you think I am?" I said. "And who do you think you are?"

Mary laughed at this.

"Seriously, Thom. Hedi thinks you're Brian Jones."

"Brian Jones is dead," I said, speaking metaphorically.

"You'd better tell Hedi that."

"I will, I will."

"Really? You'd say that?"

"Well, not the real Brian Jones is dead. The one she thinks is Brian is dead."

"But you're alive and well," she said.

"So the truth won't hurt," I said.

"The truth always hurts," she said.

"Wait a minute," I said. "You thought I'd left you forever, but I hadn't. That hurt?"

"You having a new girlfriend did."

"Hedi's not my girlfriend. I love you, Mary."

"I like Hedi," she said. "She's kind. She's a good person."

"So I should tell her the truth, that I'm not Brian Jones?"

"I think you should tell her that, yes, and Winona, too. What's the matter with you?"

Sitting knees to knees with her in that treehouse, I had the audacity to claim, ""We're just giving people what they want."

"By giving them what they don't? I think America's corrupted you."

"No it hasn't," I laughed. "It's shown us the way."

"You don't wear socks anymore," she said. "That's an improvement."

"Of course," I said, stalling.

"Look Thom, you can't run away from this forever. It's catching up with you, socks or no socks."

"I love you Mary," I said.

"So 'fess up," she insisted. "Be a man. You can do it."

"You sound like David," I said.

"That's quite a compliment," she laughed. "I

like him a lot. He's a good person and he's been my hero. I'm sure he's going to tell Winona that he's not really Keith."

"But he doesn't want to disappoint anyone either," I persisted.

"Hey, I thought the whole point of the Rolling Stones is to disenchant everyone."

She was too smart for me. I adored this woman. I had one more slingshot left: "The whole point of the Stones is to rock us to the delta, that's the truth."

"What do you know about the truth, Thom One?" and she kissed me on the cheek.

"I love you, Mary, that's the truth."

We came to an agreement. "I'd rather the whole earth would fall in and swallow me up than do what I have to do," I told her.

"Be careful what you wish for," she said.

It was later that very afternoon that I called David on the phone at the hotel where he was staying in San Francisco and told him what I was going to do. He encouraged me to do so right away.

And it was at the very moment when I called up Hedi at her uncle's place where she and

Like a Rolling Stone

Winona were staying that something snapped and an iota of my wish came true. Just as I was about to tell them the truth, the earth shook and the sea shimmered and the line disconnected.

AFTERWORD

Thom One today has four children, seven grandchildren and three great-grandchildren, all of them Americans.

David Carpenter today has one son who lives and works in America.

David and Thom were recently reunited when David wrote to Thom, asking, "Do you think about it a lot?" and Thom replied, "Every single day."

Bonus Story
Not Just Another Plot

"Writing a book, grandpa?" she asked from the back seat of the car.

"Why?" I said, catching her eye in the rear-view mirror. "What's it to you?"

"Well, a subplot is not just another plot, you know" she said. "It's an echo of the main plot."

"I know that," I said.

Rhyanwyn is 14 years old. How would she know that?

"Hemingway said it," she said.

"Really Rhy?" I said. "You're reading Hemingway?"

"We found it in the stuff at his house," said Lana, Rhyanwyn's friend, who is 15.

"I like this story where they cut each other's hair," said Rhy.

"Shorter and shorter," said Lana. "Really short."

"Interesting," I said."

Like a Rolling Stone

"Very interesting," said the girls in the back seat.

That's how we found out what was really going on.

She was ours now, Rhyanwyn, daughter of our son Gawain. She came into our lives at the age of nine, reluctantly on her part. Could we ever do enough for her? A child of the wilderness, she arrived in Key West "learning to love alone," she once told me.

Wanting to save her from herself, we tried everything. She'd have none of it. It was not dire things that happened so much as disobedience, awesome enough to leave us breathless.

How many days had she skipped school? Especially days when I myself had dropped her off and picked her up.

The cell phone we purchased for her to keep us in touch actually cut her off from us completely, linking her with a circle of friends of which we had no part. The only way we managed to keep in touch was through transportation. A bike or a bus would never get her from New Town across to the other side of the island, to the heart of Old Town, in anywhere near the time she felt she needed to get there. So we'd give her a ride.

I was never quite sure where she actually went. "We have a back way in" was what she told us. I only knew that her destination was at the far, purple end of Mullet Lane, where I dropped her off after school just about every weekday.

"Bye," I'd say each time, and each time she'd bounce out of the back seat, slam the door and canter down the lane, cell phone attached to her ear, directly to whatever mystery awaited her the other side of the gate at the end of that lane next to the Hemingway House.

I was conflicted about that gateway and she knew it. Lana was one thing, but who else hung out beyond it? She said his name was Carlos, a boy in high school. His mother owned a cottage near there, or someone in her family did, and Carlos and his gang had built tiki huts there in a "garden beyond the garden," according to Rhy.

I mean a gang in the most wholesome way. It was a good thing these kids were still in town. Rhy had only one real friendship, with Lana — and that could be turbulent — but the fact is she knew a whole pack of kids. In common with each other, they were all, unsteadily, losing their orbit around school.

Like a Rolling Stone

One time, when her class-cutting got really out of hand, I went in search of Rhy, following clues given me by Lana who had never cut a class in her life. Her pencil sketch got me to Big Pine Key, north of Key West, over 30 miles of bridges and islands and then a left turn and at last, in the countryside, an overgrown grove of campers and trailers.

At the fence I'd called Rhyanwyn's name. From a variety of windows popped the heads of several girls. Then the heads of the boys, older and with longer hair. I had blundered onto Pinocchio land. Here was where the runaways came, where they paid the rent with whatever it was they could lift from their parents' houses to pawn for cash.

To our knowledge Rhy never did visit Pinocchio Land again, once her path had slid across Carlos. The group of friends that gathered at the end of the Old Town lane next to the Hemingway House was managing somehow, mostly, to stay in school. Rhy and Lana, I guessed, were the youngest among them.

Until that day in the car when Rhy came up with her nugget about subplots, I had no idea that she'd scored a bulls-eye in our family's history.

Hemingway and me, we go way back, to school afternoons as a young idiot reading my own life revealed in Papa's writing; later only to the oceanic work not published for years, providing pleasure purely in writing, in pure writing, writing "beyond the bones of the others."

Truth, as a consequence, pierced deep. "You've been hanging out at his house all this time?" I'd asked her, back in the car.

"We swim in his pool after hours," said Lana. They squealed at this.

"You're kidding," I cut in. "Are you making this up?"

Rhy described the pool, Lana told of its temperature. They recited the story of Ernest being pissed off with his then-wife Pauline about it.

"It's you who told me about all those people," said Rhy. "Are you conflicted about this, grandpa?"

"Oh, I cannot begin to tell you," I said. "I am lost for words. We must talk."

"Turn the car around!" she commanded. "We're going back in."

"Yes!" said Lana.

Like a Rolling Stone

So I turned the car around. We arrived back at the mouth of the lane and my heart began to beat with that same strange serenity my mind felt when I first opened a book by Papa.

The girls instructed me to park at the end of the lane. Twilight was coming on fast. We snuck out of the car and the two of them crept secretly off to the right so they could open from the inside the gateway that had caused me so much inner conflict. And then we were all in the empty grounds, standing in front of that famous empty house, as different now from the crowded place that the world knew as the twilight moon is from sunlit midday.

The girls ran barefoot across the expanse of lawn. They led me by some unknowable, secret way into the master's very writing lodge itself. There I saw with my own eyes his bloated trunk with the letters E.H. stamped on its ancient hide. Then they took me into the big house itself and showed off his library shelves bent with their loads of western novels and volumes of his own books in strange languages ("Far Vail Till Vap Neu"). They took me then to his and Pauline's huge bedroom, the big bed and its carved headboard illuminated by a multitude of tall windows. Across the bedspread sprawled a great white cat. A black cat snoozed, wedged against a corner post.

The girls were at peace in this place. Rhy seemed completely at home. "What have you learned here?" I asked. Then I conflicted the whole question. "Have you learned anything?"

They unwrapped themselves from the two cats, kissed the creatures goodbye and loped off to another room on the southwest corner of the house.

A glassed-in bookcase had already been somehow penetrated by the time I got there and the girls were seated on the floor browsing through a book they'd already liberated. "This one's the best," insisted Lana.

I saw that it wasn't one of Hemingway's personal copies. This was a bright red volume wrapped in a plastic cover and it had been published years after his suicide. Lana pointed the spine at me: "The Garden of Eden."

"It's crazy," said Rhy. "He is a famous writer" — she looked at me with scorn — "and his wife wants him to bring another woman along on their honeymoon."

"Wait," laughed Lana, "that's not really it. They swim in the cove together, they eat all these meals, it's about everything..."

"Yes!" said Rhy.

"And she wants him to cut his hair like hers," said Lana, "and bleach it the same color so he doesn't know who he is."

"Then," yelled Rhy, "she burns all his writing."

"Oh, that's too bad!" I exclaimed. "Did he really deserve that?"

"He was two-minded see, Grandpa. Being of two minds is a sin."

"Ah," I said. I was still crouched on my knees between them. "You think I'm two-minded, Rhy?"

"Well, you do say you want to talk and then you say you're lost for words." She wiped her nose with the back of her hand. "It's hard when you're like that."

Lana slammed the book shut. "The cats!" she yelled.

Both of girls were up and gone before I could get to my feet. I trailed their chattering down the stairs and across the garden lawn in its evening shades of blue and black. We regrouped in a far corner of the grounds, around a small lignum vitae tree. Although wizened and wise already, such a specimen was probably quite young. "I love this tree," I said. "Of course," said Rhy.

Lana yelled "Cats!" again and all kinds of them began appearing, silently loping toward us, several of them appearing neglected and needy yet their smarts gave them away, they harbored no pretense within themselves and knew very well that they were the best-cared-for felines on the island.

"Do you want to see the house's basement?" asked Rhy.

"Nah," I said. "Too deep."

So.

Flash forward. It was weeks after that sacred evening when Rhyanwyn finally marched through our front door and, instead of retreating directly to her room, headed straight for her grandmother and me and hugged us.

We realized right then that she was leaving us.

"I love you," she said. "I want you both to know how much I love you."

"You're going to your father's?" asked her grandmother.

"He sent me a ticket," she said.

Then she looked at me and said, "Oh, why am I crying?"

Like a Rolling Stone

"Because you're of two minds, maybe?" I said.

"Grandpa," she laughed. "I'm crying because I'm happy."

And with that she left us.

About the Author

Mark Clifford Howell and his twin brother Michael Graham Howell were born in July of the last year of Hitler's life in Cheltenham Spa in the county of Gloucestershire in the United Kingdom.

Their grandfather was the mayor of Cheltenham during the Second World War. The earliest records of the family date back to 1760, with a David Howell and family living at Pen-y-myyndd, which was a hillside farm above Cwm Gwaun, near Llanychaer in Wales.

A later relative, William Griffiths Howell, born in 1846 in Llanffawer, became director of education for the Rhonnda.

The Howell twins had a brother, the late David Howell, and a sister Diana, who as Diana Lamplugh lost her eldest daughter Suzy in a presumed kidnap after which her body never found, a crime that led to a multitude of books and TV programs when Diana and her husband Paul, both awarded the Order of the British Empire, campaigned tirelessly for the cause of personal safety.

Michael and Mark attended Cheltenham College, a boarding school for boys whose true horrors are graphically on display in Lindsay Anderson's movie "If," filmed at the school that he himself attended.

Howell first came to America the year after Kennedy was killed and he got his first real job in the real world as an elevator operator in New York City, following a timely call to Conrad Hilton.

Then came three university years at Trinity College in Cambridge, a time spent largely recovering from hitchhiking trips along the hippie trails of North Africa and the Middle East. Cambridge above all was a place of the deepest friendships that have lasted a lifetime. Mark's brother Mike meanwhile began his long and successful career in catering and the hospitality industry, ultimately retiring as Secretary of the East India Club in London's St. James Square.

Armed amazingly with both a BA and MA degree in literature, Mark launched into a literary career in Montreal, Canada, appointed editor of a weekly newspaper in the now notorious Midnight stable of tabloids.

This was in the late Sixties and the publications of Joe Azaria, born in Baghdad, and his editor-in-chief John Vader quickly became more radical even than the stories they favored (like "I Watched a Wild Hog Eat My Baby!") thankfully morphing into our fave stories such as "Your Sons and Daughters Will Prophesy, Your Young Men will See Visions" —a much more accurate portrait of the time.

Family life and its responsibilities brought Howell back to London, specifically to Barnard's Inn, High Holborn, home of New English Library, the British division of New American Library, which is how Howell got to know Chevy Chase's dad, Ned Chase, the top man at NAL at the time. "I don't think my son is all that funny, do you?" "He's hilarious, Mr. Chase," is the answer Ned got every time he asked that question.

What Howell and his colleague, Laurence James, did at New English Library has become a lurid part of paperback history and made them starring figures in collector's zines such as Paperback Fanatic. Here's the late James himself in an interview reprinted in 2009 some years after his death:

"I'd only been there for 10 days and was swamped until the editorial director said to me, 'It's alright, I've got someone coming who'll help you. And I said to him, 'Well, I've never been in paperback publishing at all, ever in my life. Has this guy done a lot of paperback publishing?' He said, 'No, no, he's never worked in publishing at all.' And that was Mark Howell. And we were very good together, we were really good. We were publishing 200-odd paperbacks, 60 to 80 hardbacks monthly and we had no freelancers at all, absolutely none. We did all our own editing, we did our own proofreading, we wrote the jacket copy for all those books, just the two of us. We'd pass them to and from each other, backwards and forwards and come up with minimalist copy that would say things like, 'Two men, a town, the gold. They'll come together at rainbow's end.'

"It was great. It was one of the happiest professional times of my life, because we were left to get on with it."

Inevitably success catches up with one and Howell soon found himself senior editor of Mayflower Books, one of the multiple paperback lines of Baron Bernstein's Granada Company where he joined editors such as Nick Austin and the legendary Sonny ("Fifty Shades of Grey") Mehta earlier in their publishing careers. It was Austin who called Mark Howell the "best editorial risk-taker he'd ever met" in revealing to the press that his stint at Mayflower was a period of "coruscating creativity and high jinks," including a completely mad rewriting of 'Shield and Sword' by Vadim Kozhevnikov (collectors take note and please do send me a copy if you have one). This was the novel that led to the Soviet-era Russian film of the same name that inspired the young Vladimir Putin's ambition to join the KGB. "Mark Howell's brilliantly subversive talents were here, as elsewhere, employed to explosive effect, although as far as I know, Mr. Putin remains blissfully unaware of the Mayflower's inspirationally crazed edition."

 Howell finally immigrated to the United States in the 1970s and began the long journey to eventual citizenship (those Sixties drifts through Teheran and Kabul causing the immigration authorities literally years of heartache).

 While raising his two sons in Vermont with their mom and making a weekly commute to and from White River Junction, Howell joined Harcourt Brace Jovanovich on Madison Avenue in New York as senior editor of Pyramid Books, with Woody Allen playing clarinet in the Carlyle downstairs. There he brought to life such paperback hits as "I Was the House Dick" (as in hotel detective), no relation to

"Vasectomy and Vasectomania," one of Howell's biggest paperback hits in London.

His next step was a leap to Toronto, headquarters of Harlequin Books. The publishing queen of romance fiction had made a quantum leap herself by acquiring the rights to the duke of action adventure, Mack Bolan, hero of Don Pendleton's series "War Against the Mafia."

Harlequin's idea had some measure of mystical foresight, which was to make Mack's new enemy international terrorism. A new imprint was established for this unlikely bedmate to the romance lines. It was named Gold Eagle and Mark Howell was its first editorial director and recipient of a company car. So prescient was the choice of theme and so well were the books crafted by the best action writers in the business that President Reagan was soon rumored to be one of the series and its shoot 'em up spin-offs most devoted readers.

But the world of romance was not lost on Mark Howell as he haunted the corridors of addictive romance, perfumed, as Cole Porter once wittily observed, with the faint aroma of performing seals.

Among Harlequin's salacious truths:

Although a woman thinks she can change a man, a man never changes.

Although a man thinks a woman will not change, a woman always changes.

A man throws all his cards on the table: this is what I earn; this is what I want.

A woman keeps a couple of cards back (one of them often called Jack).

The best conversation opener is, "Where are you from?"

The best response is to listen.

A woman's best pick-up line is "Hi."

A man's response to that is to smile.

Howell's own romantic life would blossom when he moved on from Harlequin and journeyed to the very end of the road, Key West, Florida, where he met his wife Jan and joined her fabulous family with his own (see the dedication to this volume).

It was in Key West, joining the world of the *Solares Hill* newspaper with David Ethridge at the helm, that Mark Howell, as senior writer and ultimately editor of that countercultural publication, would win 17 awards from the Florida Press Club. Among the winning entries was his weekly must-read column Soundings as well as incisive interviews with world celebrities such as Mikhail Gorbachev. Howell had become, in the

Like a Rolling Stone

words of Bob Kelly's blog, "a marvelous example of the old-school reporter, furiously scribbling notes in his small, spiral-bound notepad, interjecting questions when needed but hearing the nuances of the melody behind the beat, then rushing off for one more interview before writing to deadline."

Thank you for reading.
Please review this book. Reviews help others find Absolutely Amazing eBooks and inspire us to keep providing these marvelous tales.

If you would like to be put on our email list to receive updates on new releases, contests, and promotions, please go to AbsolutelyAmazingEbooks.com and sign up.

The New Atlantian Library

NewAtlantianLibrary.com
or AbsolutelyAmazingeBooks.com
or AA-eBooks.com

www.ingramcontent.com/pod-product-compliance
Lightning Source LLC
Chambersburg PA
CBHW050841160426
43192CB00011B/2106